MznLnx

Missing Links Exam Preps

Exam Prep for

Essentials of Strategic Management, The Quest for Competitive Advantage

Gamble & Thompson, Jr., 1st Edition

The MznLnx Exam Prep is your link from the texbook and lecture to your exams.
The MznLnx Exam Preps are unauthorized and comprehensive reviews of your textbooks.

All material provided by MznLnx and Rico Publications (c) 2010
Textbook publishers and textbook authors do not particpate in or contribute to these reviews.

MznLnx

Rico
Publications

Exam Prep for Essentials of Strategic Management, The Quest for Competitive Advantage
1st Edition
Gamble & Thompson, Jr.

Publisher: Raymond Houge
Assistant Editor: Michael Rouger
Text and Cover Designer: Lisa Buckner
Marketing Manager: Sara Swagger
Project Manager, Editorial Production: Jerry Emerson
Art Director: Vernon Lowerui

Product Manager: Dave Mason
Editorial Assitant: Rachel Guzmanji
Pedagogy: Debra Long
Cover Image: Jim Reed/Getty Images
Text and Cover Printer: City Printing, Inc.
Compositor: Media Mix, Inc.

(c) 2010 Rico Publications
ALL RIGHTS RESERVED. No part of this work covered by the copyright may be reproduced or used in any form or by an means--graphic, electronic, or mechanical, including photocopying, recording, taping, Web distribution, information storage, and retrieval systems, or in any other manner--without the written permission of the publisher.

Printed in the United States
ISBN:

For more information about our products, contact us at:
Dave.Mason@RicoPublications.com

For permission to use material from this text or product, submit a request online to:
Dave.Mason@RicoPublications.com

Contents

CHAPTER 1
Strategy and the Quest for Competitive Advantage   1

CHAPTER 2
Leadership and the Strategic Management Process   5

CHAPTER 3
Competitive Strategy and Advantage in the Marketplace   10

CHAPTER 4
Industry and Competitive Analysis   13

CHAPTER 5
Analyzing a Company`s Competitive Strength and Cost Structure   18

CHAPTER 6
Superior Strategy Execution—Another Path to Competitive Advantage   22

CHAPTER 7
Ethical Business Strategies, Corporate Social Responsibility, and Environment   30

CHAPTER 8
Strategies for Competing in International Markets   34

CHAPTER 9
Strategies for Multibusiness Corporations   40

ANSWER KEY   45

TO THE STUDENT

COMPREHENSIVE

The *MznLnx* Exam Prep series is designed to help you pass your exams. Editors at MznLnx review your textbooks and then prepare these practice exams to help you master the textbook material. Unlike study guides, workbooks, and practice tests provided by the texbook publisher and textbook authors, *MznLnx* gives you **all** of the material in each chapter in exam form, not just samples, so you can be sure to nail your exam.

MECHANICAL

The MznLnx Exam Prep series creates exams that will help you learn the subject matter as well as test you on your understanding. Each question is designed to help you master the concept. Just working through the exams, you gain an understanding of the subject--its a simple mechanical process that produces success.

INTEGRATED STUDY GUIDE AND REVIEW

MznLnx is not just a set of exams designed to test you, its also a comprehensive review of the subject content. Each exam question is also a review of the concept, making sure that you will get the answer correct without having to go to other sources of material. You learn as you go! Its the easiest way to pass an exam.

HUMOR

Studying can be tedious and dry. MznLnx's instructional design includes moderate humor within the exam questions on occassion, to break the tedium and revitalize the brain

Chapter 1. Strategy and the Quest for Competitive Advantage

1. A _____ is a framework for creating economic, social, and/or other forms of value. The term _____ is thus used for a broad range of informal and formal descriptions to represent core aspects of a business, including purpose, offerings, strategies, infrastructure, organizational structures, trading practices, and operational processes and policies.

Conceptualizations of _____s try to formalize informal descriptions into building blocks and their relationships.

   a. Gap analysis
   b. Business model design
   c. Business networking
   d. Business model

2. _____ of the learning curve effect and the closely related experience curve effect express the relationship between equations for experience and efficiency or between efficiency gains and investment in the effort. The experience of 'learning curves' was first observed by the 19th Century German psychologist Hermann Ebbinghaus according to the difficulty of memorizing varying numbers of verbal stimuli, and subsequent learning about the complex processes of learning are discussed in the

.

The rule used for representing the learning curve effect states that the more times a task has been performed, the less time will be required on each subsequent iteration.

   a. Spatial Decision Support Systems
   b. Distribution
   c. Point biserial correlation coefficient
   d. Models

3. _____ is, in very basic words, a position a firm occupies against its competitors.

According to Michael Porter, the three methods for creating a sustainable _____ are through:

1. Cost leadership

2. Differentiation

3. Focus (economics)

a. Theory Z
b. 1990 Clean Air Act
c. 28-hour day
d. Competitive advantage

4. A _____ is a formal relationship between two or more parties to pursue a set of agreed upon goals or to meet a critical business need while remaining independent organizations.

Partners may provide the _____ with resources such as products, distribution channels, manufacturing capability, project funding, capital equipment, knowledge, expertise, or intellectual property. The alliance is a cooperation or collaboration which aims for a synergy where each partner hopes that the benefits from the alliance will be greater than those from individual efforts.

a. Farmshoring
b. Golden parachute
c. Process automation
d. Strategic alliance

5. Competitive advantage is, in very basic words, a position a firm occupies against its competitors.

According to Michael Porter, the three methods for creating a _____ are through:

1. Cost leadership - Cost advantage occurs when a firm delivers the same services as its competitors but at a lower cost;

2.

a. 1990 Clean Air Act
b. Theory Z
c. 28-hour day
d. Sustainable competitive advantage

6. A _____ is a name or trademark connected with a product or producer. _____s have become increasingly important components of culture and the economy, now being described as 'cultural accessories and personal philosophies'.

Some people distinguish the psychological aspect of a _____ from the experiential aspect.

a. Brand extension
b. Brand awareness
c. Brand loyalty
d. Brand

7. A niche market is the subset of the market on which a specific product is focusing on; Therefore the _____ defines the specific product features aimed at satisfying specific market needs, as well as the price range, production quality and the demographics that is intended to impact.

Every single product that is on sale can be defined by its niche market. As of special note, the products aimed at a wide demographics audience, with the resulting low price (due to Price elasticity of demand), are said to belong to the Mainstream niche, in practice referred only as Mainstream or of high demand.

a. Prevailing wage
b. Labor intensive
c. Dominant logic
d. Market niche

8. A _____ or transnational corporation is a corporation or enterprise that manages production or delivers services in more than one country. It can also be referred to as an international corporation.

The first modern _____ is generally thought to be the Dutch East India Company, established in 1602.

a. Command center
b. Small and medium enterprises
c. Financial Accounting Standards Board
d. Multinational corporation

9. A _____ is a concept used in strategic management that groups companies within an industry that have similar business models or similar combinations of strategies. For example, the restaurant industry can be divided into several _____s including fast-food and fine-dining based on variables such as preparation time, pricing, and presentation. The number of groups within an industry and their composition depends on the dimensions used to define the groups.
a. Corporate strategy
b. Strategic business unit
c. Strategic drift
d. Strategic group

10. An _____ is a mostly hierarchical concept of subordination of entities that collaborate and contribute to serve one common aim.

Organizations are a variant of clustered entities. The structure of an organization is usually set up in many a styles, dependent on their objectives and ambience.

   a. Organizational development
   b. Informal organization
   c. Open shop
   d. Organizational structure

Chapter 2. Leadership and the Strategic Management Process 5

1. An _____ is a person who has possession of an enterprise and assumes significant accountability for the inherent risks and the outcome. It is an ambitious leader who combines land, labor, and capital to create and market new goods or services. The term is a loanword from French and was first defined by the Irish economist Richard Cantillon.
    a. AAAI
    b. Entrepreneur
    c. A Stake in the Outcome
    d. A4e

2. _____ has been described as the 'process of social influence in which one person can enlist the aid and support of others in the accomplishment of a common task'. A definition more inclusive of followers comes from Alan Keith of Genentech who said '_____ is ultimately about creating a way for people to contribute to making something extraordinary happen.'

    _____ is one of the most salient aspects of the organizational context. However, defining _____ has been challenging.

    a. Leadership
    b. Situational leadership
    c. 28-hour day
    d. 1990 Clean Air Act

3. _____ refers to the methods of practicing and using another person's business philosophy. The franchisor grants the independent operator the right to distribute its products, techniques, and trademarks for a percentage of gross monthly sales and a royalty fee. Various tangibles and intangibles such as national or international advertising, training, and other support services are commonly made available by the franchisor.
    a. 28-hour day
    b. Franchising
    c. ServiceMaster
    d. 1990 Clean Air Act

4. A _____ is a brief written statement of the purpose of a company or organization. Ideally, a _____ guides the actions of the organization, spells out its overall goal, provides a sense of direction, and guides decision making for all levels of management.

    _____s often contain the following:

    - Purpose and aim of the organization
    - The organization's primary stakeholders: clients, stockholders, etc.
    - Responsibilities of the organization toward these stakeholders
    - Products and services offered

Chapter 2. Leadership and the Strategic Management Process

In developing a _____:

- Encourage as much input as feasible from employees, volunteers, and other stakeholders
- Publicize it broadly

The _____ can be used to resolve differences between business stakeholders. Stakeholders include: employees including managers and executives, stockholders, board of directors, customers, suppliers, distributors, creditors, governments (local, state, federal, etc.), unions, competitors, NGO's, and the general public.

a. 1990 Clean Air Act
b. 28-hour day
c. 33 Strategies of War
d. Mission statement

5. The _____ is a performance management tool for measuring whether the smaller-scale operational activities of a company are aligned with its larger-scale objectives in terms of vision and strategy.

By focusing not only on financial outcomes but also on the operational, marketing and developmental inputs to these, the _____ helps provide a more comprehensive view of a business, which in turn helps organizations act in their best long-term interests. This tool is also being used to address business response to climate change and greenhouse gas emissions.

a. Middle management
b. Management development
c. Commercial management
d. Balanced scorecard

6. In economics, _____s are key economic variables that economists used to predict a new phase of the business cycle. A _____ is one that changes before the economy does; a lagging indicator is one that changes after the economy has changed. Examples of _____s include stock prices, which often improve or worsen before a similar change in the economy.

a. Leading indicator
b. Deflation
c. Human capital
d. Perfect competition

7. _____ is the set of processes, customs, policies, laws, and institutions affecting the way a corporation (or company) is directed, administered or controlled. _____ also includes the relationships among the many stakeholders involved and the goals for which the corporation is governed. The principal stakeholders are the shareholders/members, management, and the board of directors.
   a. Flextime
   b. Guarantee
   c. Corporate governance
   d. No-FEAR Act

8. _____ is a form of corporate self-regulation integrated into a business model. Ideally, _____ policy would function as a built-in, self-regulating mechanism whereby business would monitor and ensure their adherence to law, ethical standards, and international norms. Business would embrace responsibility for the impact of their activities on the environment, consumers, employees, communities, stakeholders and all other members of the public sphere.
   a. 33 Strategies of War
   b. Corporate social responsibility
   c. 1990 Clean Air Act
   d. 28-hour day

9. A _____ is a framework for creating economic, social, and/or other forms of value. The term _____ is thus used for a broad range of informal and formal descriptions to represent core aspects of a business, including purpose, offerings, strategies, infrastructure, organizational structures, trading practices, and operational processes and policies.

Conceptualizations of _____s try to formalize informal descriptions into building blocks and their relationships.

   a. Business networking
   b. Business model
   c. Gap analysis
   d. Business model design

10. _____ of the learning curve effect and the closely related experience curve effect express the relationship between equations for experience and efficiency or between efficiency gains and investment in the effort. The experience of 'learning curves' was first observed by the 19th Century German psychologist Hermann Ebbinghaus according to the difficulty of memorizing varying numbers of verbal stimuli, and subsequent learning about the complex processes of learning are discussed in the

.

The rule used for representing the learning curve effect states that the more times a task has been performed, the less time will be required on each subsequent iteration.

a. Point biserial correlation coefficient
b. Spatial Decision Support Systems
c. Distribution
d. Models

11. Organizational culture is not the same as _____. It is wider and deeper concepts, something that an organization 'is' rather than what it 'has' (according to Buchanan and Huczynski.)

_____ is the total sum of the values, customs, traditions and meanings that make a company unique.

a. Job analysis
b. Corporate culture
c. Work design
d. Path-goal theory

12. _____ is a form of applied ethics that examines ethical principles and moral or ethical problems that arise in a business environment. It applies to all aspects of business conduct and is relevant to the conduct of individuals and business organizations as a whole. Applied ethics is a field of ethics that deals with ethical questions in many fields such as medical, technical, legal and _____.
a. Hypernorms
b. Corporate Sustainability
c. Facilitation payments
d. Business ethics

13. A _____ is a body of elected or appointed members who jointly oversee the activities of a company or organization. The body sometimes has a different name, such as board of trustees, board of governors, board of managers, or executive board. It is often simply referred to as 'the board.'

A board's activities are determined by the powers, duties, and responsibilities delegated to it or conferred on it by an authority outside itself.

a. Competition law
b. Clean Water Act
c. Foreign Corrupt Practices Act
d. Board of directors

14. The _____ duty is a legal relationship of confidence or trust between two or more parties, most commonly a _____ or trustee and a principal or beneficiary. One party, for example a corporate trust company or the trust department of a bank, holds a _____ relation or acts in a _____ capacity to another, such as one whose funds are entrusted to it for investment. In a _____ relation one person justifiably reposes confidence, good faith, reliance and trust in another whose aid, advice or protection is sought in some matter.

   a. Copyright Act of 1976
   b. Last Injurious Exposure Rule
   c. Corporate governance
   d. Fiduciary

15. _____ is the self-government of a nation, country or some portion thereof, generally exercising sovereignty.

The term _____ is used in contrast to subjugation, which refers to a region as a 'territory' --subject to the political and military control of an external government. The word is sometimes used in a weaker sense to contrast with hegemony, the indirect control of one nation by another, more powerful nation.

   a. A Stake in the Outcome
   b. AAAI
   c. A4e
   d. Independence

Chapter 3. Competitive Strategy and Advantage in the Marketplace

1. _____ is, in very basic words, a position a firm occupies against its competitors.

According to Michael Porter, the three methods for creating a sustainable _____ are through:

1. Cost leadership

2. Differentiation

3. Focus (economics)

   a. 1990 Clean Air Act
   b. Theory Z
   c. 28-hour day
   d. Competitive advantage

2. A _____ is a formal relationship between two or more parties to pursue a set of agreed upon goals or to meet a critical business need while remaining independent organizations.

Partners may provide the _____ with resources such as products, distribution channels, manufacturing capability, project funding, capital equipment, knowledge, expertise, or intellectual property. The alliance is a cooperation or collaboration which aims for a synergy where each partner hopes that the benefits from the alliance will be greater than those from individual efforts.

   a. Process automation
   b. Farmshoring
   c. Golden parachute
   d. Strategic alliance

3. In marketing, _____ has come to mean the process by which marketers try to create an image or identity in the minds of their target market for its product, brand, or organization. It is the 'relative competitive comparison' their product occupies in a given market as perceived by the target market.

Re-_____ involves changing the identity of a product, relative to the identity of competing products, in the collective minds of the target market.

   a. PEST analysis
   b. Context analysis
   c. Customer analytics
   d. Positioning

Chapter 3. Competitive Strategy and Advantage in the Marketplace

4. A niche market is the subset of the market on which a specific product is focusing on; Therefore the _____ defines the specific product features aimed at satisfying specific market needs, as well as the price range, production quality and the demographics that is intended to impact.

Every single product that is on sale can be defined by its niche market. As of special note, the products aimed at a wide demographics audience, with the resulting low price (due to Price elasticity of demand), are said to belong to the Mainstream niche, in practice referred only as Mainstream or of high demand.

   a. Labor intensive
   b. Prevailing wage
   c. Dominant logic
   d. Market niche

5. A _____ or transnational corporation is a corporation or enterprise that manages production or delivers services in more than one country. It can also be referred to as an international corporation.

The first modern _____ is generally thought to be the Dutch East India Company, established in 1602.

   a. Command center
   b. Multinational corporation
   c. Financial Accounting Standards Board
   d. Small and medium enterprises

6. A _____ is a concept used in strategic management that groups companies within an industry that have similar business models or similar combinations of strategies. For example, the restaurant industry can be divided into several _____s including fast-food and fine-dining based on variables such as preparation time, pricing, and presentation. The number of groups within an industry and their composition depends on the dimensions used to define the groups.
   a. Corporate strategy
   b. Strategic business unit
   c. Strategic drift
   d. Strategic group

7. Organizational culture is not the same as _____. It is wider and deeper concepts, something that an organization 'is' rather than what it 'has' (according to Buchanan and Huczynski.)

_____ is the total sum of the values, customs, traditions and meanings that make a company unique.

a. Job analysis
b. Path-goal theory
c. Work design
d. Corporate culture

8. _____ is a concept related to the relative abilities of parties in a situation to exert influence over each other. If both parties are on an equal footing in a debate, then they will have equal _____, such as in a perfectly competitive market, or between an evenly matched monopoly and monopsony.

There are a number of fields where the concept of _____ has proven crucial to coherent analysis: game theory, labour economics, collective bargaining arrangements, diplomatic negotiations, settlement of litigation, the price of insurance, and any negotiation in general.

a. Bargaining power
b. Trade credit
c. 1990 Clean Air Act
d. Buy-sell agreement

9. _____ is something that a firm can do well and that meets the following three conditions:

Competencies are things that companys execute well across several business units or product sectors.

Firms usually have few competencies, but these are usually less liable to change rapidly.

1. It provides consumer benefits
2. It is not easy for competitors to imitate
3. It can be leveraged widely to many products and markets.

A _____ can take various forms, including technical/subject matter know-how, a reliable process and/or close relationships with customers and suppliers (Mascarenhas et al. 1998.)

a. Dominant Design
b. Learning-by-doing
c. NAIRU
d. Core competency

1. In economics and sociology, an _____ is any factor (financial or non-financial) that enables or motivates a particular course of action, or counts as a reason for preferring one choice to the alternatives. It is an expectation that encourages people to behave in a certain way. Since human beings are purposeful creatures, the study of _____ structures is central to the study of all economic activity (both in terms of individual decision-making and in terms of co-operation and competition within a larger institutional structure.)
   a. Incentive
   b. AAAI
   c. A Stake in the Outcome
   d. A4e

2. An _____ is a formal scheme used to promote or encourage specific actions or behavior by a specific group of people during a defined period of time. _____s are particularly used in business management to motivate employees, and in sales in order to attract and retain customers. The scientific literature also refers to this concept as Pay for Performance.
   a. A Stake in the Outcome
   b. AAAI
   c. A4e
   d. Incentive program

3. _____ is a concept related to the relative abilities of parties in a situation to exert influence over each other. If both parties are on an equal footing in a debate, then they will have equal _____, such as in a perfectly competitive market, or between an evenly matched monopoly and monopsony.

   There are a number of fields where the concept of _____ has proven crucial to coherent analysis: game theory, labour economics, collective bargaining arrangements, diplomatic negotiations, settlement of litigation, the price of insurance, and any negotiation in general.

   a. Trade credit
   b. 1990 Clean Air Act
   c. Buy-sell agreement
   d. Bargaining power

4. _____ is a strategic planning method used to evaluate the Strengths, Weaknesses, Opportunities, and Threats involved in a project or in a business venture. It involves specifying the objective of the business venture or project and identifying the internal and external factors that are favorable and unfavorable to achieving that objective. The technique is credited to Albert Humphrey, who led a convention at Stanford University in the 1960s and 1970s using data from Fortune 500 companies.

a. SWOT analysis
b. Corporate image
c. Marketing
d. Market share

5. A _____ is a type of business entity in which partners (owners) share with each other the profits or losses of the business. _____s are often favored over corporations for taxation purposes, as the _____ structure does not generally incur a tax on profits before it is distributed to the partners (i.e. there is no dividend tax levied.) However, depending on the _____ structure and the jurisdiction in which it operates, owners of a _____ may be exposed to greater personal liability than they would as shareholders of a corporation.

a. Mediation
b. Due process
c. Federal Employers Liability Act
d. Partnership

6. A _____ is a formal relationship between two or more parties to pursue a set of agreed upon goals or to meet a critical business need while remaining independent organizations.

Partners may provide the _____ with resources such as products, distribution channels, manufacturing capability, project funding, capital equipment, knowledge, expertise, or intellectual property. The alliance is a cooperation or collaboration which aims for a synergy where each partner hopes that the benefits from the alliance will be greater than those from individual efforts.

a. Strategic alliance
b. Process automation
c. Golden parachute
d. Farmshoring

7. A _____ is a name or trademark connected with a product or producer. _____s have become increasingly important components of culture and the economy, now being described as 'cultural accessories and personal philosophies'.

Some people distinguish the psychological aspect of a _____ from the experiential aspect.

a. Brand extension
b. Brand awareness
c. Brand
d. Brand loyalty

Chapter 4. Industry and Competitive Analysis

8. _____, in microeconomics, are the cost advantages that a business obtains due to expansion. They are factors that cause a producer's average cost per unit to fall as scale is increased. _____ is a long run concept and refers to reductions in unit cost as the size of a facility, or scale, increases.

   a. Economies of scale
   b. A4e
   c. Economies of scope
   d. A Stake in the Outcome

9. _____ in its literal sense is the process of transformation of local or regional phenomena into global ones. It can be described as a process by which the people of the world are unified into a single society and function together.

This process is a combination of economic, technological, sociocultural and political forces.

   a. Histogram
   b. Collaborative Planning, Forecasting and Replenishment
   c. Cost Management
   d. Globalization

10. _____ or _____ data refers to selected population characteristics as used in government, marketing or opinion research, or the _____ profiles used in such research. Note the distinction from the term 'demography' Commonly-used _____s include race, age, income, disabilities, mobility (in terms of travel time to work or number of vehicles available), educational attainment, home ownership, employment status, and even location.

   a. Demographic
   b. Abraham Harold Maslow
   c. Affiliation
   d. Adam Smith

11. A _____ is a process in which a potential employee is evaluated by an employer for prospective employment in their company, organization and was established in the late 16th century.

A _____ typically precedes the hiring decision, and is used to evaluate the candidate. The interview is usually preceded by the evaluation of submitted résumés from interested candidates, then selecting a small number of candidates for interviews.

   a. Split shift
   b. Job interview
   c. Supported employment
   d. Payrolling

Chapter 4. Industry and Competitive Analysis

12. A _____ is a concept used in strategic management that groups companies within an industry that have similar business models or similar combinations of strategies. For example, the restaurant industry can be divided into several _____s including fast-food and fine-dining based on variables such as preparation time, pricing, and presentation. The number of groups within an industry and their composition depends on the dimensions used to define the groups.
   a. Strategic business unit
   b. Strategic drift
   c. Corporate strategy
   d. Strategic group

13. A broad definition of _____ is the action of gathering, analyzing, and distributing information about products, customers, competitors and any aspect of the environment needed to support executives and managers in making strategic decisions for an organization.

Key points of this definitions:

   1. _____ is an ethical and legal business practice. (This is important as _____ professionals emphasize that the discipline is not the same as industrial espionage which is both unethical and usually illegal.)
   2. The focus is on the external business environment.
   3. There is a process involved in gathering information, converting it into intelligence and then utilizing this in business decision making. _____ professionals emphasize that if the intelligence gathered is not usable (or actionable) then it is not intelligence.

A more focused definition of _____ regards it as the organizational function responsible for the early identification of risks and opportunities in the market before they become obvious. Experts also call this process the early signal analysis. This definition focuses attention on the difference between dissemination of widely available factual information (such as market statistics, financial reports, newspaper clippings) performed by functions such as libraries and information centers, and _____ which is a perspective on developments and events aimed at yielding a competitive edge.

   a. Competitive intelligence
   b. 28-hour day
   c. 1990 Clean Air Act
   d. Competitor or Competitive Intelligence

14. _____ is a form of applied ethics that examines ethical principles and moral or ethical problems that arise in a business environment. It applies to all aspects of business conduct and is relevant to the conduct of individuals and business organizations as a whole. Applied ethics is a field of ethics that deals with ethical questions in many fields such as medical, technical, legal and _____.

a. Facilitation payments
b. Hypernorms
c. Business ethics
d. Corporate Sustainability

Chapter 5. Analyzing a Company's Competitive Strength and Cost Structure

1. The _____ is a concept from business management that was first described and popularized by Michael Porter in his 1985 best-seller, Competitive Advantage: Creating and Sustaining Superior Performance.

A _____ is a chain of activities. Products pass through all activities of the chain in order and at each activity the product gains some value. The chain of activities gives the products more added value than the sum of added values of all activities. It is important not to mix the concept of the _____ with the costs occurring throughout the activities.

   a. Value chain
   b. Customer relationship management
   c. Mass marketing
   d. Market development

2. In finance, a _____ or accounting ratio is a ratio of two selected numerical values taken from an enterprise's financial statements. There are many standard ratios used to try to evaluate the overall financial condition of a corporation or other organization. _____s may be used by managers within a firm, by current and potential shareholders (owners) of a firm, and by a firm's creditors.
   a. Rate of return
   b. Return on equity
   c. Return on sales
   d. Financial ratio

3. _____ is a strategic planning method used to evaluate the Strengths, Weaknesses, Opportunities, and Threats involved in a project or in a business venture. It involves specifying the objective of the business venture or project and identifying the internal and external factors that are favorable and unfavorable to achieving that objective. The technique is credited to Albert Humphrey, who led a convention at Stanford University in the 1960s and 1970s using data from Fortune 500 companies.
   a. SWOT analysis
   b. Corporate image
   c. Marketing
   d. Market share

4. In economics, business, retail, and accounting, a _____ is the value of money that has been used up to produce something, and hence is not available for use anymore. In economics, a _____ is an alternative that is given up as a result of a decision. In business, the _____ may be one of acquisition, in which case the amount of money expended to acquire it is counted as _____.

Chapter 5. Analyzing a Company`s Competitive Strength and Cost Structure

a. Cost overrun
b. Cost allocation
c. Fixed costs
d. Cost

5. _____ is a marketing strategy 'in which one firm tries to distinguish its product or service from competing products on the basis of attributes like design and workmanship' (McConnell-Brue, 2002, p. 437-438). The firm can also distinguish its product offering through quality of service, extensive distribution, customer focus, or any other sustainable competitive advantage other than price. It can be contrasted with price competition, which is where a company tries to distinguish its product or service from competing products on the basis of low price.

a. 33 Strategies of War
b. 1990 Clean Air Act
c. 28-hour day
d. Non-price competition

6. _____ is the process of comparing the cost, cycle time, productivity, or quality of a specific process or method to another that is widely considered to be an industry standard or best practice. Essentially, _____ provides a snapshot of the performance of your business and helps you understand where you are in relation to a particular standard. The result is often a business case for making changes in order to make improvements.

a. Cost leadership
b. Competitive heterogeneity
c. Complementors
d. Benchmarking

7. _____ is a costing model that identifies activities in an organization and assigns the cost of each activity resource to all products and services according to the actual consumption by each: it assigns more indirect costs (overhead) into direct costs.

In this way an organization can establish the true cost of its individual products and services for the purposes of identifying and eliminating those which are unprofitable and lowering the prices of those which are overpriced.

In a business organization, the ABC methodology assigns an organization's resource costs through activities to the products and services provided to its customers.

a. A Stake in the Outcome
b. A4e
c. Indirect costs
d. Activity-based costing

Chapter 5. Analyzing a Company's Competitive Strength and Cost Structure

8. In management accounting, _____ establishes budget and actual cost of operations, processes, departments or product and the analysis of variances, profitability or social use of funds. Managers use _____ to support decision-making to cut a company's costs and improve profitability. As a form of management accounting, _____ need not follow standards such as GAAP, because its primary use is for internal managers, rather than outside users, and what to compute is instead decided pragmatically.
   a. Transaction cost
   b. Quality costs
   c. Marginal cost
   d. Cost accounting

9. _____ is a concept related to the relative abilities of parties in a situation to exert influence over each other. If both parties are on an equal footing in a debate, then they will have equal _____, such as in a perfectly competitive market, or between an evenly matched monopoly and monopsony.

   There are a number of fields where the concept of _____ has proven crucial to coherent analysis: game theory, labour economics, collective bargaining arrangements, diplomatic negotiations, settlement of litigation, the price of insurance, and any negotiation in general.

   a. 1990 Clean Air Act
   b. Bargaining power
   c. Buy-sell agreement
   d. Trade credit

10. In microeconomics and management, the term _____ describes a style of management control. Vertically integrated companies are united through a hierarchy with a common owner. Usually each member of the hierarchy produces a different product or (market-specific) service, and the products combine to satisfy a common need.
    a. 1990 Clean Air Act
    b. 28-hour day
    c. 33 Strategies of War
    d. Vertical integration

11. _____ is subcontracting a process, such as product design or manufacturing, to a third-party company. The decision to outsource is often made in the interest of lowering cost or making better use of time and energy costs, redirecting or conserving energy directed at the competencies of a particular business, or to make more efficient use of land, labor, capital, (information) technology and resources. _____ became part of the business lexicon during the 1980s.

Chapter 5. Analyzing a Company's Competitive Strength and Cost Structure

a. Unemployment insurance
b. Outsourcing
c. Opinion leadership
d. Operant conditioning

12.   A _____ is a formal relationship between two or more parties to pursue a set of agreed upon goals or to meet a critical business need while remaining independent organizations.

Partners may provide the _____ with resources such as products, distribution channels, manufacturing capability, project funding, capital equipment, knowledge, expertise, or intellectual property. The alliance is a cooperation or collaboration which aims for a synergy where each partner hopes that the benefits from the alliance will be greater than those from individual efforts.

a. Farmshoring
b. Golden parachute
c. Strategic alliance
d. Process automation

13.   _____ is, in very basic words, a position a firm occupies against its competitors.

According to Michael Porter, the three methods for creating a sustainable _____ are through:

1. Cost leadership

2. Differentiation

3. Focus (economics)

a. 1990 Clean Air Act
b. Theory Z
c. 28-hour day
d. Competitive advantage

Chapter 6. Superior Strategy Execution—Another Path to Competitive Advantage

1. Organizational culture is not the same as _____. It is wider and deeper concepts, something that an organization 'is' rather than what it 'has' (according to Buchanan and Huczynski.)

   _____ is the total sum of the values, customs, traditions and meanings that make a company unique.

   a. Path-goal theory
   b. Work design
   c. Job analysis
   d. Corporate culture

2. _____ refers to the stock of skills and knowledge embodied in the ability to perform labor so as to produce economic value. It is the skills and knowledge gained by a worker through education and experience. Many early economic theories refer to it simply as labor, one of three factors of production, and consider it to be a fungible resource -- homogeneous and easily interchangeable.
   a. Deflation
   b. Market structure
   c. Productivity management
   d. Human capital

3. _____ is a strategic planning method used to evaluate the Strengths, Weaknesses, Opportunities, and Threats involved in a project or in a business venture. It involves specifying the objective of the business venture or project and identifying the internal and external factors that are favorable and unfavorable to achieving that objective. The technique is credited to Albert Humphrey, who led a convention at Stanford University in the 1960s and 1970s using data from Fortune 500 companies.
   a. Market share
   b. Corporate image
   c. Marketing
   d. SWOT analysis

4. _____ has been described as the 'process of social influence in which one person can enlist the aid and support of others in the accomplishment of a common task' . A definition more inclusive of followers comes from Alan Keith of Genentech who said '_____ is ultimately about creating a way for people to contribute to making something extraordinary happen.'

   _____ is one of the most salient aspects of the organizational context. However, defining _____ has been challenging.

Chapter 6. Superior Strategy Execution—Another Path to Competitive Advantage

a. Situational leadership
b. Leadership
c. 28-hour day
d. 1990 Clean Air Act

5. An _____ is a mostly hierarchical concept of subordination of entities that collaborate and contribute to serve one common aim.

Organizations are a variant of clustered entities. The structure of an organization is usually set up in many a styles, dependent on their objectives and ambience.

a. Organizational development
b. Open shop
c. Informal organization
d. Organizational structure

6. The _____ is a concept from business management that was first described and popularized by Michael Porter in his 1985 best-seller, Competitive Advantage: Creating and Sustaining Superior Performance.

A _____ is a chain of activities. Products pass through all activities of the chain in order and at each activity the product gains some value. The chain of activities gives the products more added value than the sum of added values of all activities. It is important not to mix the concept of the _____ with the costs occurring throughout the activities.

a. Mass marketing
b. Market development
c. Value chain
d. Customer relationship management

7. _____ refers to increasing the spiritual, political, social or economic strength of individuals and communities. It often involves the empowered developing confidence in their own capacities.

The term Human _____ covers a vast landscape of meanings, interpretations, definitions and disciplines ranging from psychology and philosophy to the highly commercialized Self-Help industry and Motivational sciences.

a. AAAI
b. Empowerment
c. A Stake in the Outcome
d. A4e

8. _____ is used to assign the available resources in an economic way. It is part of resource management.

In strategic planning, is a plan for using available resources, for example human resources, especially in the near term, to achieve goals for the future.

a. 1990 Clean Air Act
b. 28-hour day
c. 33 Strategies of War
d. Resource allocation

9. _____ are a set of documents that describe an organization's policies for operation and the procedures necessary to fulfill the policies. They are often initiated because of some external requirement, such as environmental compliance or other governmental regulations, such as the American Sarbanes-Oxley Act requiring full openness in accounting practices. The easiest way to start writing _____ is to interview the users of the _____ and create a flow chart or task map or work flow of the process from start to finish.

a. Customer retention
b. Horizontal integration
c. Group booking
d. Policies and procedures

10. _____ is a form of applied ethics that examines ethical principles and moral or ethical problems that arise in a business environment. It applies to all aspects of business conduct and is relevant to the conduct of individuals and business organizations as a whole. Applied ethics is a field of ethics that deals with ethical questions in many fields such as medical, technical, legal and _____.

a. Hypernorms
b. Facilitation payments
c. Business ethics
d. Corporate Sustainability

11. _____, in microeconomics, are the cost advantages that a business obtains due to expansion. They are factors that cause a producer's average cost per unit to fall as scale is increased. _____ is a long run concept and refers to reductions in unit cost as the size of a facility, or scale, increases.

a. A4e
b. A Stake in the Outcome
c. Economies of scope
d. Economies of scale

12. Network externalities resemble economies of scale, but they are not considered such because they are a function of the number of users of a good or service in an industry, not of the production efficiency within a business. _____ are only considered examples of network externalities if they are driven by demand side economies.

Formally, a production function f is defined to have:

- constant returns to scale if (for any constant a greater than or equal to 0) $f(aK, aL) = af(K, L)$
- increasing returns to scale if (for any constant a greater than 1) $f(aK, aL) > af(K, L)$
- decreasing returns to scale if (for any constant a greater than 1) $f(aK, aL) < af(K, L)$

where K and L are factors of production, capital and labour, respectively.

As an example, the Cobb-Douglas functional form has constant returns to scale when the sum of the exponents adds up to one.

a. AAAI
b. Economies of scale external to the firm
c. A Stake in the Outcome
d. A4e

13. _____ is the process of comparing the cost, cycle time, productivity, or quality of a specific process or method to another that is widely considered to be an industry standard or best practice. Essentially, _____ provides a snapshot of the performance of your business and helps you understand where you are in relation to a particular standard. The result is often a business case for making changes in order to make improvements.
a. Cost leadership
b. Benchmarking
c. Complementors
d. Competitive heterogeneity

Chapter 6. Superior Strategy Execution—Another Path to Competitive Advantage

14. A _____ or business method is a collection of related, structured activities or tasks that produce a specific service or product (serve a particular goal) for a particular customer or customers. It often can be visualized with a flowchart as a sequence of activities.

There are three types of _____ es:

1. Management processes, the processes that govern the operation of a system. Typical management processes include 'Corporate Governance' and 'Strategic Management'.
2. Operational processes, processes that constitute the core business and create the primary value stream. Typical operational processes are Purchasing, Manufacturing, Marketing, and Sales.
3. Supporting processes, which support the core processes. Examples include Accounting, Recruitment, Technical support.

A _____ begins with a customer's need and ends with a customer's need fulfillment. Process oriented organizations break down the barriers of structural departments and try to avoid functional silos.

   a. Business process
   b. 28-hour day
   c. 1990 Clean Air Act
   d. 33 Strategies of War

15. _____ is, in computer science and management, an approach aiming at improvements by means of elevating efficiency and effectiveness of the business process that exist within and across organizations. The key to _____ is for organizations to look at their business processes from a 'clean slate' perspective and determine how they can best construct these processes to improve how they conduct business. _____ Cycle.

_____ is also known as _____, Business Process Redesign, Business Transformation, or Business Process Change Management.

   a. Horizontal integration
   b. Business process reengineering
   c. Personal management interview
   d. Product life cycle

16. In probability theory, a probability distribution is called _____ if its cumulative distribution function is _____. This is equivalent to saying that for random variables X with the distribution in question, Pr[X = a] = 0 for all real numbers a, i.e.: the probability that X attains the value a is zero, for any number a. If the distribution of X is _____ then X is called a _____ random variable.

a. Decision tree pruning
b. Pay Band
c. Connectionist expert systems
d. Continuous

17. _____ is a management process whereby delivery (customer valued) processes are constantly evaluated and improved in the light of their efficiency, effectiveness and flexibility.

Some see it as a meta process for most management systems (Business Process Management, Quality Management, Project Management). Deming saw it as part of the 'system' whereby feedback from the process and customer were evaluated against organisational goals.

a. Continuous Improvement Process
b. Critical Success Factor
c. Sole proprietorship
d. First-mover advantage

18. _____ is a business management strategy, initially implemented by Motorola, that today enjoys widespread application in many sectors of industry.

_____ seeks to improve the quality of process outputs by identifying and removing the causes of defects (errors) and variation in manufacturing and business processes. It uses a set of quality management methods, including statistical methods, and creates a special infrastructure of people within the organization ('Black Belts' etc.)

a. Theory of constraints
b. Takt time
c. Production line
d. Six sigma

19. _____ is a business management strategy aimed at embedding awareness of quality in all organizational processes. _____ has been widely used in manufacturing, education, hospitals, call centers, government, and service industries, as well as NASA space and science programs.

Chapter 6. Superior Strategy Execution—Another Path to Competitive Advantage

As defined by the International Organization for Standardization (ISO):

'_____ is a management approach for an organization, centered on quality, based on the participation of all its members and aiming at long-term success through customer satisfaction, and benefits to all members of the organization and to society.' ISO 8402:1994

One major aim is to reduce variation from every process so that greater consistency of effort is obtained. (Royse, D., Thyer, B., Padgett D., ' Logan T., 2006)

a. 1990 Clean Air Act
b. 28-hour day
c. Quality management
d. Total quality management

20. _____ is one of the managerial functions like planning, organizing, staffing and directing. It is an important function because it helps to check the errors and to take the corrective action so that deviation from standards are minimized and stated goals of the organization are achieved in desired manner. According to modern concepts, _____ is a foreseeing action whereas earlier concept of _____ was used only when errors were detected. _____ in management means setting standards, measuring actual performance and taking corrective action.
a. Schedule of reinforcement
b. Control
c. Turnover
d. Decision tree pruning

21. In engineering and manufacturing, _____ and quality engineering are used in developing systems to ensure products or services are designed and produced to meet or exceed customer requirements. Refer to the definition by Merriam-Webster for further information. These systems are often developed in conjunction with other business and engineering disciplines using a cross-functional approach.
a. Quality control
b. Process capability
c. Statistical process control
d. Single Minute Exchange of Die

22. _____ can be considered to have three main components: quality control, quality assurance and quality improvement. _____ is focused not only on product quality, but also the means to achieve it. _____ therefore uses quality assurance and control of processes as well as products to achieve more consistent quality.

Chapter 6. Superior Strategy Execution—Another Path to Competitive Advantage

a. 28-hour day
b. Quality management
c. Total quality management
d. 1990 Clean Air Act

23. In economics and sociology, an _____ is any factor (financial or non-financial) that enables or motivates a particular course of action, or counts as a reason for preferring one choice to the alternatives. It is an expectation that encourages people to behave in a certain way. Since human beings are purposeful creatures, the study of _____ structures is central to the study of all economic activity (both in terms of individual decision-making and in terms of co-operation and competition within a larger institutional structure.)

a. A4e
b. AAAI
c. A Stake in the Outcome
d. Incentive

24. _____ refers to the process of screening, and selecting qualified people for a job at an organization or firm mid- and large-size organizations and companies often retain professional recruiters or outsource some of the process to _____ agencies. External _____ is the process of attracting and selecting employees from outside the organization.

The _____ industry has four main types of agencies: employment agencies, _____ websites and job search engines, 'headhunters' for executive and professional _____, and in-house _____.

a. Labour hire
b. Recruitment Process Outsourcing
c. Referral recruitment
d. Recruitment

Chapter 7. Ethical Business Strategies, Corporate Social Responsibility, and Environment

1. _____ is a form of applied ethics that examines ethical principles and moral or ethical problems that arise in a business environment. It applies to all aspects of business conduct and is relevant to the conduct of individuals and business organizations as a whole. Applied ethics is a field of ethics that deals with ethical questions in many fields such as medical, technical, legal and _____.

    a. Hypernorms
    b. Business ethics
    c. Facilitation payments
    d. Corporate Sustainability

2. _____, in microeconomics, are the cost advantages that a business obtains due to expansion. They are factors that cause a producer's average cost per unit to fall as scale is increased. _____ is a long run concept and refers to reductions in unit cost as the size of a facility, or scale, increases.

    a. Economies of scope
    b. Economies of scale
    c. A4e
    d. A Stake in the Outcome

3. Network externalities resemble economies of scale, but they are not considered such because they are a function of the number of users of a good or service in an industry, not of the production efficiency within a business. _____ are only considered examples of network externalities if they are driven by demand side economies.

Formally, a production function $\ $ is defined to have:

- constant returns to scale if (for any constant a greater than or equal to 0) $\ $
- increasing returns to scale if (for any constant a greater than 1) $\ $
- decreasing returns to scale if (for any constant a greater than 1) $\ $

where K and L are factors of production, capital and labour, respectively.

As an example, the Cobb-Douglas functional form has constant returns to scale when the sum of the exponents adds up to one.

   a. Economies of scale external to the firm
   b. AAAI
   c. A Stake in the Outcome
   d. A4e

Chapter 7. Ethical Business Strategies, Corporate Social Responsibility, and Environment

4. _____ has been described as the 'process of social influence in which one person can enlist the aid and support of others in the accomplishment of a common task' . A definition more inclusive of followers comes from Alan Keith of Genentech who said '_____ is ultimately about creating a way for people to contribute to making something extraordinary happen.'

_____ is one of the most salient aspects of the organizational context. However, defining _____ has been challenging.

   a. Situational leadership
   b. 1990 Clean Air Act
   c. 28-hour day
   d. Leadership

5. Organizational culture is not the same as _____. It is wider and deeper concepts, something that an organization 'is' rather than what it 'has' (according to Buchanan and Huczynski.)

_____ is the total sum of the values, customs, traditions and meanings that make a company unique.

   a. Corporate culture
   b. Job analysis
   c. Work design
   d. Path-goal theory

6. In philosophy _____ is the position that moral or ethical propositions do not reflect objective and/or universal moral truths, but instead make claims relative to social, cultural, historical or personal circumstances. Moral relativists hold that no universal standard exists by which to assess an ethical proposition's truth. Relativistic positions often see moral values as applicable only within certain cultural boundaries (cultural relativism) or in the context of individual preferences (individualist ethical subjectivism.)
   a. Moral absolutism
   b. Moral relativism
   c. 28-hour day
   d. 1990 Clean Air Act

7. _____ is a form of corporate self-regulation integrated into a business model. Ideally, _____ policy would function as a built-in, self-regulating mechanism whereby business would monitor and ensure their adherence to law, ethical standards, and international norms. Business would embrace responsibility for the impact of their activities on the environment, consumers, employees, communities, stakeholders and all other members of the public sphere.

Chapter 7. Ethical Business Strategies, Corporate Social Responsibility, and Environment

a. 33 Strategies of War
b. 28-hour day
c. 1990 Clean Air Act
d. Corporate social responsibility

8. _____ is a business approach that creates long-term shareholder value by embracing opportunities and managing risks deriving from economic, environmental and social developments.

_____ is an evolution on more traditional phrases describing ethical corporate practice. Phrases such as corporate social responsibility or corporate citizenship continue to be used but are increasingly superseded by the broader term, _____.

a. Sexual harassment
b. 1990 Clean Air Act
c. 28-hour day
d. Corporate sustainability

9. The 'business case for _____', theorizes that in a global marketplace, a company that employs a diverse workforce (both men and women, people of many generations, people from ethnically and racially diverse backgrounds etc.) is better able to understand the demographics of the marketplace it serves and is thus better equipped to thrive in that marketplace than a company that has a more limited range of employee demographics.

An additional corollary suggests that a company that supports the _____ of its workforce can also improve employee satisfaction, productivity and retention.

a. Kanban
b. Trademark
c. Virtual team
d. Diversity

10. The _____ is the labour pool in employment. It is generally used to describe those working for a single company or industry, but can also apply to a geographic region like a city, country, state, etc. The term generally excludes the employers or management, and implies those involved in manual labour.
a. Work-life balance
b. Pink-collar worker
c. Division of labour
d. Workforce

Chapter 7. Ethical Business Strategies, Corporate Social Responsibility, and Environment

11. _____ refers to the process of screening, and selecting qualified people for a job at an organization or firm mid- and large-size organizations and companies often retain professional recruiters or outsource some of the process to _____ agencies. External _____ is the process of attracting and selecting employees from outside the organization.

The _____ industry has four main types of agencies: employment agencies, _____ websites and job search engines, 'headhunters' for executive and professional _____, and in-house _____.

a. Recruitment Process Outsourcing
b. Labour hire
c. Referral recruitment
d. Recruitment

Chapter 8. Strategies for Competing in International Markets

1. _____ is something that a firm can do well and that meets the following three conditions:

Competencies are things that companys execute well across several business units or product sectors.

Firms usually have few competencies, but these are usually less liable to change rapidly.

   1. It provides consumer benefits
   2. It is not easy for competitors to imitate
   3. It can be leveraged widely to many products and markets.

A _____ can take various forms, including technical/subject matter know-how, a reliable process and/or close relationships with customers and suppliers (Mascarenhas et al. 1998.)

   a. Learning-by-doing
   b. NAIRU
   c. Dominant Design
   d. Core competency

2. _____ or _____ data refers to selected population characteristics as used in government, marketing or opinion research, or the _____ profiles used in such research. Note the distinction from the term 'demography' Commonly-used _____s include race, age, income, disabilities, mobility (in terms of travel time to work or number of vehicles available), educational attainment, home ownership, employment status, and even location.
   a. Abraham Harold Maslow
   b. Adam Smith
   c. Affiliation
   d. Demographic

3. In economics, business, retail, and accounting, a _____ is the value of money that has been used up to produce something, and hence is not available for use anymore. In economics, a _____ is an alternative that is given up as a result of a decision. In business, the _____ may be one of acquisition, in which case the amount of money expended to acquire it is counted as _____.
   a. Fixed costs
   b. Cost overrun
   c. Cost allocation
   d. Cost

4. _____ is the process of comparing the cost, cycle time, productivity, or quality of a specific process or method to another that is widely considered to be an industry standard or best practice. Essentially, _____ provides a snapshot of the performance of your business and helps you understand where you are in relation to a particular standard. The result is often a business case for making changes in order to make improvements.

a. Complementors
b. Benchmarking
c. Competitive heterogeneity
d. Cost leadership

5. In finance, the _____s between two currencies specifies how much one currency is worth in terms of the other. It is the value of a foreign nation's currency in terms of the home nation's currency. For example an _____ of 102 Japanese yen to the United States dollar means that JPY 102 is worth the same as USD 1.
   a. A4e
   b. A Stake in the Outcome
   c. Exchange rate
   d. AAAI

6. _____ is a strategic planning method used to evaluate the Strengths, Weaknesses, Opportunities, and Threats involved in a project or in a business venture. It involves specifying the objective of the business venture or project and identifying the internal and external factors that are favorable and unfavorable to achieving that objective. The technique is credited to Albert Humphrey, who led a convention at Stanford University in the 1960s and 1970s using data from Fortune 500 companies.
   a. SWOT analysis
   b. Marketing
   c. Corporate image
   d. Market share

7. _____ is exchange of capital, goods, and services across international borders or territories. In most countries, it represents a significant share of gross domestic product (GDP.) While _____ has been present throughout much of history, its economic, social, and political importance has been on the rise in recent centuries.
   a. A4e
   b. A Stake in the Outcome
   c. AAAI
   d. International trade

8. In finance, an _____ is a contract between a buyer and a seller that gives the buyer the right--but not the obligation--to buy or to sell a particular asset (the underlying asset) at a later day at an agreed price. In return for granting the _____, the seller collects a payment (the premium) from the buyer. A call _____ gives the buyer the right to buy the underlying asset; a put _____ gives the buyer of the _____ the right to sell the underlying asset.

a. A4e
b. AAAI
c. A Stake in the Outcome
d. Option

9. _____ refers to the methods of practicing and using another person's business philosophy. The franchisor grants the independent operator the right to distribute its products, techniques, and trademarks for a percentage of gross monthly sales and a royalty fee. Various tangibles and intangibles such as national or international advertising, training, and other support services are commonly made available by the franchisor.
a. 1990 Clean Air Act
b. 28-hour day
c. ServiceMaster
d. Franchising

10. _____ is a concept related to the relative abilities of parties in a situation to exert influence over each other. If both parties are on an equal footing in a debate, then they will have equal _____, such as in a perfectly competitive market, or between an evenly matched monopoly and monopsony.

There are a number of fields where the concept of _____ has proven crucial to coherent analysis: game theory, labour economics, collective bargaining arrangements, diplomatic negotiations, settlement of litigation, the price of insurance, and any negotiation in general.

a. Trade credit
b. Buy-sell agreement
c. 1990 Clean Air Act
d. Bargaining power

11. _____ as defined in business terms is an organization's strategic guide to globalization. A sound _____ should address these questions: what must be (versus what is) the extent of market presence in the world's major markets? How to build the necessary global presence? What must be (versus what is) the optimal locations around the world for the various value chain activities? How to run global presence into global competitive advantage?

Academic research on _____ came of age during the 1980s, including work by Michael Porter and Christopher Bartlett ' Sumantra Ghoshal. Among the forces perceived to bring about the globalization of competition were convergence in economic systems and technological change, especially in information technology, that facilitated and required the coordination of a multinational firm's strategy on a worldwide scale.

a. 28-hour day
b. Global strategy
c. 33 Strategies of War
d. 1990 Clean Air Act

12. A _____ is a formal relationship between two or more parties to pursue a set of agreed upon goals or to meet a critical business need while remaining independent organizations.

Partners may provide the _____ with resources such as products, distribution channels, manufacturing capability, project funding, capital equipment, knowledge, expertise, or intellectual property. The alliance is a cooperation or collaboration which aims for a synergy where each partner hopes that the benefits from the alliance will be greater than those from individual efforts.

a. Process automation
b. Farmshoring
c. Golden parachute
d. Strategic alliance

13. In decision theory and estimation theory, the _____ of an estimator, $\hat{\theta}$, of an unknown parameter of the distribution, θ, is the expected value of the loss function

$$R(\theta, \hat{\theta}) = \mathbb{E}_\theta L(\theta, \hat{\theta}) = \int L(\theta, \hat{\theta})\, dP_\theta.$$

where dP_θ is a probability measure parametrized by θ.

- For a scalar parameter θ and a quadratic loss function,

$$L(\theta, \hat{\theta}) = (\theta - \hat{\theta})^2$$

the _____ function becomes the mean squared error of the estimate,

$$R(\theta, \hat{\theta}) = E_\theta(\theta - \hat{\theta})^2$$

- In density estimation, the unknown parameter is probability density itself. The loss function is typically chosen to be a norm in an appropriate function space. For example, for L^2 norm,

$$L(f, \hat{f}) = \|f - \hat{f}\|_2^2$$

the _____ function becomes the mean integrated squared error

$$R(f, \hat{f}) = E\|f - \hat{f}\|^2$$

a. Risk
b. Financial modeling
c. Linear model
d. Risk aversion

14. _____ has been described as the 'process of social influence in which one person can enlist the aid and support of others in the accomplishment of a common task'. A definition more inclusive of followers comes from Alan Keith of Genentech who said '_____ is ultimately about creating a way for people to contribute to making something extraordinary happen.'

_____ is one of the most salient aspects of the organizational context. However, defining _____ has been challenging.

a. Leadership
b. 28-hour day
c. Situational leadership
d. 1990 Clean Air Act

Chapter 8. Strategies for Competing in International Markets

15. A _____ or transnational corporation is a corporation or enterprise that manages production or delivers services in more than one country. It can also be referred to as an international corporation.

The first modern _____ is generally thought to be the Dutch East India Company, established in 1602.

   a. Command center
   b. Financial Accounting Standards Board
   c. Small and medium enterprises
   d. Multinational corporation

16. An _____ is a person temporarily or permanently residing in a country and culture other than that of the person's upbringing or legal residence. The word comes from the Latin ex and patria (country, fatherland.)

The term is sometimes used in the context of Westerners living in non-Western countries, although it is also used to describe Westerners living in other Western countries, such as Americans living in the United Kingdom, or Britons living in Spain.

   a. AAAI
   b. Expatriate
   c. A Stake in the Outcome
   d. A4e

17. _____, in microeconomics, are the cost advantages that a business obtains due to expansion. They are factors that cause a producer's average cost per unit to fall as scale is increased. _____ is a long run concept and refers to reductions in unit cost as the size of a facility, or scale, increases.

   a. A Stake in the Outcome
   b. A4e
   c. Economies of scope
   d. Economies of scale

Chapter 9. Strategies for Multibusiness Corporations

1. The phrase mergers and _____s refers to the aspect of corporate strategy, corporate finance and management dealing with the buying, selling and combining of different companies that can aid, finance, or help a growing company in a given industry grow rapidly without having to create another business entity.

   An _____, also known as a takeover or a buyout, is the buying of one company (the 'target') by another. An _____ may be friendly or hostile.

   a. A Stake in the Outcome
   b. Acquisition
   c. AAAI
   d. A4e

2. A mutual _____ or stockholder is an individual or company (including a corporation) that legally owns one or more shares of stock in a joint stock company. A company's _____s collectively own that company. Thus, the typical goal of such companies is to enhance _____ value.
   a. Stockholder
   b. Free riding
   c. Shareholder
   d. 1990 Clean Air Act

3. _____ is a business buzz term, which implies that the ultimate measure of a company's success is to enrich shareholders. It became popular during the 1980s, and is particularly associated with former CEO of General Electric, Jack Welch. In March 2009, Welch openly turned his back on the concept, calling _____ 'the dumbest idea in the world'.
   a. Gross profit margin
   b. Corporate finance
   c. Sweat equity
   d. Shareholder value

4. A _____ is an entity formed between two or more parties to undertake economic activity together. The parties agree to create a new entity by both contributing equity, and they then share in the revenues, expenses, and control of the enterprise. The venture can be for one specific project only, or a continuing business relationship such as the Fuji Xerox _____.
   a. Civil Rights Act of 1991
   b. Patent
   c. Meritor Savings Bank v. Vinson
   d. Joint venture

5. A _____ is a formal relationship between two or more parties to pursue a set of agreed upon goals or to meet a critical business need while remaining independent organizations.

Chapter 9. Strategies for Multibusiness Corporations 41

Partners may provide the _____ with resources such as products, distribution channels, manufacturing capability, project funding, capital equipment, knowledge, expertise, or intellectual property. The alliance is a cooperation or collaboration which aims for a synergy where each partner hopes that the benefits from the alliance will be greater than those from individual efforts.

- a. Farmshoring
- b. Golden parachute
- c. Process automation
- d. Strategic alliance

6. An _____ is a person who has possession of an enterprise and assumes significant accountability for the inherent risks and the outcome. It is an ambitious leader who combines land, labor, and capital to create and market new goods or services. The term is a loanword from French and was first defined by the Irish economist Richard Cantillon.
- a. AAAI
- b. Entrepreneur
- c. A Stake in the Outcome
- d. A4e

7. The _____ is a concept from business management that was first described and popularized by Michael Porter in his 1985 best-seller, Competitive Advantage: Creating and Sustaining Superior Performance.

A _____ is a chain of activities. Products pass through all activities of the chain in order and at each activity the product gains some value. The chain of activities gives the products more added value than the sum of added values of all activities. It is important not to mix the concept of the _____ with the costs occurring throughout the activities.

- a. Market development
- b. Customer relationship management
- c. Mass marketing
- d. Value chain

8. In economics, business, retail, and accounting, a _____ is the value of money that has been used up to produce something, and hence is not available for use anymore. In economics, a _____ is an alternative that is given up as a result of a decision. In business, the _____ may be one of acquisition, in which case the amount of money expended to acquire it is counted as _____.

a. Fixed costs
b. Cost allocation
c. Cost overrun
d. Cost

9. _____ is the process of comparing the cost, cycle time, productivity, or quality of a specific process or method to another that is widely considered to be an industry standard or best practice. Essentially, _____ provides a snapshot of the performance of your business and helps you understand where you are in relation to a particular standard. The result is often a business case for making changes in order to make improvements.
   a. Complementors
   b. Cost leadership
   c. Competitive heterogeneity
   d. Benchmarking

10. A _____ is a name or trademark connected with a product or producer. _____s have become increasingly important components of culture and the economy, now being described as 'cultural accessories and personal philosophies'.

Some people distinguish the psychological aspect of a _____ from the experiential aspect.

   a. Brand awareness
   b. Brand loyalty
   c. Brand
   d. Brand extension

11. _____, in microeconomics, are the cost advantages that a business obtains due to expansion. They are factors that cause a producer's average cost per unit to fall as scale is increased. _____ is a long run concept and refers to reductions in unit cost as the size of a facility, or scale, increases.
   a. A Stake in the Outcome
   b. Economies of scope
   c. A4e
   d. Economies of scale

12. _____ are conceptually similar to economies of scale. Whereas economies of scale primarily refer to efficiencies associated with supply-side changes, such as increasing or decreasing the scale of production, of a single product type, _____ refer to efficiencies primarily associated with demand-side changes, such as increasing or decreasing the scope of marketing and distribution, of different types of products. _____ are one of the main reasons for such marketing strategies as product bundling, product lining, and family branding.

Chapter 9. Strategies for Multibusiness Corporations

a. Economies of scope
b. A4e
c. A Stake in the Outcome
d. Economies of scale

13. In finance and economics, _____ or divestiture is the reduction of some kind of asset for either financial or ethical objectives or sale of an existing business by a firm. A _____ is the opposite of an investment.
   a. 1990 Clean Air Act
   b. Divestment
   c. 33 Strategies of War
   d. 28-hour day

14. _____ has been described as the 'process of social influence in which one person can enlist the aid and support of others in the accomplishment of a common task' . A definition more inclusive of followers comes from Alan Keith of Genentech who said '_____ is ultimately about creating a way for people to contribute to making something extraordinary happen.'

_____ is one of the most salient aspects of the organizational context. However, defining _____ has been challenging.

   a. 28-hour day
   b. 1990 Clean Air Act
   c. Leadership
   d. Situational leadership

15. In business, a _____ is a product or a business unit that generates unusually high profit margins: so high that it is responsible for a large amount of a company's operating profit. This profit far exceeds the amount necessary to maintain the _____ business, and the excess is used by the business for other purposes.

A firm is said to be acting as a _____ when its earnings per share (EPS) is equal to its dividends per share (DPS), or in other words, when a firm pays out 100% of its free cash flow (FCF) to its shareholders as dividends at the end of each accounting term.

   a. Workflow
   b. Design management in organization
   c. Cash cow
   d. Middle management

Chapter 9. Strategies for Multibusiness Corporations

16. _____ is used to assign the available resources in an economic way. It is part of resource management.

In strategic planning,is a plan for using available resources, for example human resources, especially in the near term, to achieve goals for the future.

- a. 1990 Clean Air Act
- b. 28-hour day
- c. 33 Strategies of War
- d. Resource allocation

17. A _____ is a new organization or entity formed by a split from a larger one, such as a television series based on a pre-existing one, or a new company formed from a university research group or business incubator. In literature, especially in milieu-based popular fictional book series like mysteries, westerns, fantasy or science fiction, the term sub-series is generally used instead of _____, but with essentially the same meaning.

_____s as a descriptive term can also include a dissenting faction of a membership organization, a sect of a cult, or a denomination of a church.

- a. Spin-off
- b. 33 Strategies of War
- c. 1990 Clean Air Act
- d. 28-hour day

18. _____ is the corporate management term for the act of reorganizing the legal, ownership, operational, or other structures of a company for the purpose of making it more profitable, or better organized for its present needs. Alternate reasons for _____ include a change of ownership or ownership structure, demerger repositioning debt _____ and financial _____.

- a. Restructuring
- b. Net worth
- c. Market value added
- d. Market value

ANSWER KEY

Chapter 1
1. d　　2. d　　3. d　　4. d　　5. d　　6. d　　7. d　　8. d　　9. d　　10. d

Chapter 2
1. b　　2. a　　3. b　　4. d　　5. d　　6. a　　7. c　　8. b　　9. b　　10. d
11. b　　12. d　　13. d　　14. d　　15. d

Chapter 3
1. d　　2. d　　3. d　　4. d　　5. b　　6. d　　7. d　　8. a　　9. d

Chapter 4
1. a　　2. d　　3. d　　4. a　　5. d　　6. a　　7. c　　8. a　　9. d　　10. a
11. b　　12. d　　13. a　　14. c

Chapter 5
1. a　　2. d　　3. a　　4. d　　5. d　　6. d　　7. d　　8. d　　9. b　　10. d
11. b　　12. c　　13. d

Chapter 6
1. d　　2. d　　3. d　　4. b　　5. d　　6. c　　7. b　　8. d　　9. d　　10. c
11. d　　12. b　　13. b　　14. a　　15. b　　16. d　　17. a　　18. d　　19. d　　20. b
21. a　　22. b　　23. d　　24. d

Chapter 7
1. b　　2. b　　3. a　　4. d　　5. a　　6. b　　7. d　　8. d　　9. d　　10. d
11. d

Chapter 8
1. d　　2. d　　3. d　　4. b　　5. c　　6. a　　7. d　　8. d　　9. d　　10. d
11. b　　12. d　　13. a　　14. a　　15. d　　16. b　　17. d

Chapter 9
1. b　　2. c　　3. d　　4. d　　5. d　　6. b　　7. d　　8. d　　9. d　　10. c
11. d　　12. a　　13. b　　14. c　　15. c　　16. d　　17. a　　18. a

www.ingramcontent.com/pod-product-compliance
Lightning Source LLC
Chambersburg PA
CBHW080744250426
43671CB00038B/2864